D0627682

THE FIVE
RETIREMENT
MYTHS

BY PATRICK KELLY

Cover and Interior Design by The Impact Partnership

ISBN 978-0-9833615-3-4

Printed in the USA

TO LEVI

WELCOME TO THE FAMILY

TABLE OF CONTENTS —————

THE **RETIREMENT REALITY**

PREFACE ————————————————————

Today's retirement space is noisy. Very noisy. Voices are shouting from every direction, all of them saying the same thing, "Listen to me! I've got the answer!"

That presents a challenge. While some of these messages are valuable — able to lead you to a safe, happy, and prosperous retirement — others are just noise. And quite frankly, it's often hard to tell the two apart. But what if you could? What if you were able to distinguish which of these voices were really looking out for your best interest and which were simply after their own? That would be a breath of fresh air.

In this little book, I will attempt just that. And I'm going to do it a bit differently. Instead of highlighting the messages you should listen to, I'm going to reveal five messages you should not listen to. These are messages that carry a ring of truth but sadly can lead you off-base, messages I call Retirement Myths — because, in my opinion, that's exactly what they are.

Interestingly enough, all five Retirement Myths sprout from the same branch — a branch that desperately needs pruning (or possibly complete eradication) from an individual's retirement plan in order to reap a more successful harvest in the future.

So with that little introduction, let's jump into the first of the five Retirement Myths.

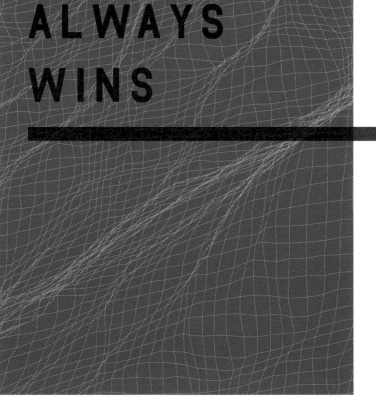

MYTH 1

BUY AND HOLD ALWAYS WINS

MYTH 1

In my book *The Retirement Miracle*, I made this statement: "Buy and hold is dead." I believed it then, but I am even more convinced today.

We live in a frantic, information-crazed world. One in which this year's business leader can become next year's bankruptcy headline, leaving its stockholders penniless in the process.

For instance, do the names Bear Stearns or Lehman Brothers (long-time darlings of Wall Street), ring a bell? They were 85- and 158-year-old companies, respectively, whose stock valuations climbed as high as $172 and $86 a share — giving these two companies a combined market capitalization of nearly $86 billion.[1] Yet, almost overnight, these two corporate titans were wiped off the financial map thanks to the colossal banking crisis, which erupted in full force during the fall of 2008; and in that one, rapid implosion, their stocks became virtually worthless. Think about that! Hundred-year-old companies worth billions of dollars gone in a night's sleep!

And they're not alone. There are hundreds of examples. And most have nothing to do with a worldwide financial crisis, but rather aggressive competition, newer technology, or even their own missteps. How about these names? Montgomery Ward. Polaroid. Mervyn's. Circuit City. Pontiac. Hollywood Video. Kodak. Enron. WorldCom. The death toll of companies that once led their industries is staggering. As a matter of fact, according to one article, only 14% of all the 1955 Fortune 500 companies are still alive today. In other words, 86% of these companies are no longer in business![II]

How have the valuations of those companies fared? (Yes, that *is* a rhetorical question.) Their ticker symbols no longer even exist.

But a company doesn't have to fail in order for its share price to plummet in value. All it has to do is lose its edge. Get beat by a competitor. Forfeit its leadership position. As you're likely aware, an industry leader generally garners tremendous value, but if it falls to second, third, or fourth place, the stock will likely suffer.

So, what's the point? Simply the obvious, or what *should* be obvious. If a majority of all businesses fail, as talked about in the article referenced on the previous page by Eli Radke, or eventually lose their leadership positions, how smart is it to simply buy today's good companies and hold onto their stocks forever? That sounds like a potential for disaster. It may have proved wise decades ago, when companies were fewer, competition was less fierce, and information moved at a snail's pace, but, today, I believe it is an antiquated strategy rife with hazards.

But, you may counter with, "Well, what if I just buy today's great companies' stocks and then sell them before they start to deteriorate in value? That should work, right?" In theory, maybe; but, it's much trickier than it sounds. For instance, how do you know when that transformation is going to occur? In today's fast-paced, 24/7 world of electronic trading, the average consumer, like you and me, is usually the last to find out — and often after crippling losses.

"Okay," you say. "Maybe picking individual companies is fraught with hazard. I'll just buy and hold index mutual funds or Exchange Traded Funds. That's always worked over the long-term!"

In truth, it has usually worked — at least so far to date and at least in the United States. As I write this, the S&P 500 index has just come off its all-time high of 2,090.57 on December 29, 2014, according to Google Finance. That means, at least in theory, if an individual purchased an index fund participating in the S&P 500 any time previous to December 29, 2014, the value of those shares at the end of 2014 would likely have been worth more than the original purchase price.[III] But did you notice the two caveats above? "At least so far to date," and "at least in the United States." Those are two enormous caveats. Let me explain.

As I was writing my second book, *The Retirement Miracle*, I searched for what I believed to be the worst-performing stock index in a major, first-world economy, over a long period of time. One index stood out quickly: Japan's Nikkei 225 index. Much like the S&P 500, the Nikkei 225 is a compilation of 225 stocks of large Japanese companies listed in the First Section of the Tokyo Stock Exchange. This benchmark index reached its all-time high on December 31, 1989 at 38,915.90 points. Twenty years later, on December 31, 2009, the value of that index was still languishing at 10,546.44 points. A massive 73-percent loss.[IV] Wow! How did that "buy and hold" strategy work out for anyone who held this index over that 20-year period?[V]

Now, let me be clear. Just because something occurred previously does not, in any way, mean it will happen again. I am not saying the S&P 500's future is doomed or that we will experience the same dismal market consequences as

Japan. In regard to future market movements, I am certain of only one thing: no one knows! And, I mean no one. The future direction of our market, as well as any other market in the world, is a mystery to all. Some may claim to know or claim to have tools that help them deduce when a market might turn, but truly, no one really knows until it has actually happened. Hindsight in the markets is always 20/20, but foresight is more like 20/400. In other words, legally blind.

My primary reason for bringing Japan's index into this discussion is to point out that indexes, even major indexes from world-leading economies, don't *always* go up. Even over long periods of time. They can lose money, and sometimes, as in the case of the Nikkei 225, a lot of money.

So, if buying both individual companies, as well as stock indexes, presents challenges to the long-espoused "buy and hold" strategy, due to the potential for loss, what is the answer? Well, I've got good news. There *is* an answer! An answer that can put the "buy and hold" strategy solidly on the path of success. And that answer is quite simple: don't lose money!

If you could simply find a way to hold onto stock index investments for the long haul, yet never lose money when that particular index went down in value, that would be the only way to know with certainty that a long-term "buy and hold" strategy would work in your favor.

The good news is there *is* such a way, with some of today's financial products, to do just that. To participate in a strategy that still offers growth potential but protects against losses. A strategy that can allow you, maybe for the first time ever, to feel confident that the long-espoused plan of "buy and hold" can work for you and help get you to your desired retirement goals.

So, sit back, read on, and see what other myths you may have been falsely holding onto as truth.

YOU CAN'T MAKE BIG RETURNS WITHOUT TAKING BIG RISKS

MYTH 2 ————————————————————

Sometimes, it's hard to let old paradigms die. And one that sits at the top of the "difficult to change" list is our belief about money and how to manage our personal finances.

And one of the erroneous, long-held paradigms I've seen falsely espoused for years is the "either/or" mentality when it comes to risk and reward. In my opinion, most individuals believe they only have two, problem-fraught options to choose from:

Option 1 – keep my money safe by putting it into a CD or savings account, and, consequently, settle for a low rate of return not currently keeping pace with inflation.[VI]

Option 2 – try to make inflation-beating returns by putting my money at risk in the equities markets.

In other words, many individuals believe that in order to receive inflation-beating returns, they must put their money at risk. But luckily, that isn't necessarily true – at least not today – due to some of the marketplace's new financial innovations. I believe it's an old paradigm that must die.

The real key to making a solid, long-term, inflation-beating return isn't in taking big risks; rather, it's primarily fueled by eliminating potential losses. And, if you can protect your downside against loss, while at the same time not give up your potential for gains, that can be a game-changer.

But you may be thinking, "Yeah, but where does that exist?"

My answer, "I'm glad you're reading this little book!"

To illustrate just how powerful this strategy can be, let's take a look, once again, at the Nikkei 225 index I spoke about in the previous chapter. If you remember, I said that over a 20-year period, from December 31, 1989 to December 31, 2009, that index was down a total of 73 percent. But what I didn't tell you was how it got there.

During that 20-year period, the Nikkei index had 11 years of losses, but it also had nine years of gains. And some of those gains were very significant. As a matter of fact, four of those nine years of gains were 19 percent or greater. Check these out:

1999 – +36.79%
2003 – +24.45%
2005 – +40.24%
2009 – +19.04%[VII]

Wow! A 40-percent gain in a single calendar year! That's incredible. Who wouldn't be happy with that kind of a return? But, unfortunately, the losses in the negative years more than wiped out those amazing gains in the positive years, dragging the total return of this index to a dismal 73-percent loss over a 20-year period.

Again, to put this into perspective, $1,000 invested into the Nikkei 225 index on December 29, 1989 (the last trading day of 1989) would only have been worth $271.01 20 years later, on December 31, 2009, even with nine years of gains along the way. See figure 2.1.

The Value of $1,000 in the Nikkei 225 from 12/31/1989 to 12/31/2009

YEAR	END OF YEAR CLOSE	ANNUAL RETURN	VALUE OF $1,000
1989	38915.90	NA	$1,000.00
1990	23,848.70	-38.72	$612.83
1991	22,983.80	-3.63	$590.60
1992	16,925.00	-26.36	$434.91
1993	17,417.20	2.91	$447.56
1994	19,723.10	13.24	$506.81
1995	19,868.20	0.74	$510.54
1996	19,361.30	-2.55	$497.52
1997	15,258.70	-21.19	$392.09
1998	13,842.17	-9.28	$355.69
1999	18,934.34	36.79	$486.55
2000	13,785.69	-27.19	$354.24
2001	10,542.60	-23.53	$270.91
2002	8,578.95	-18.63	$220.45
2003	10,676.60	24.45	$274.35
2004	11,488.76	7.61	$295.22
2005	16,111.43	40.24	$414.01
2006	17,225.83	6.92	$442.64
2007	15,307.78	-11.13	$393.36
2008	8,859.56	-42.12	$227.66
2009	10,564.44	19.04	$271.01

FIGURE 2.1

The reason protecting against loss is so important is because when your portfolio experiences losses, your growth years may simply work to get you back to where you began. It's the old "two steps forward, three steps back" conundrum. And that's no fun when it comes to your money, especially when your golden years depend on it.

So, let's play around with this a little bit and see what

effect making one little, hypothetical change would have. Let's look at this same index, but this time let's eliminate all 11 years of loss, simply making the return zero percent — no loss or no gain. Let's see what that does to the total return over the same 20-year period.

Nikkei 225 Index Removing All Loss Years

YEAR	INDEX VALUE	GAIN OR LOSS	VALUE AT YEAR END
1989	38915.9	NA	$1,000.00
1990	23848.7	0.00	$1,000.00
1991	22983.8	0.00	$1,000.00
1992	16925	0.00	$1,000.00
1993	17417.2	2.91	$1,029.08
1994	19723.1	13.24	$1,165.32
1995	19868.2	0.74	$1,173.90
1996	19361.3	0.00	$1,173.90
1997	15258.7	0.00	$1,173.90
1998	13842.17	0.00	$1,173.90
1999	18934.34	36.79	$1,605.74
2000	13785.69	0.00	$1,605.74
2001	10542.6	0.00	$1,605.74
2002	8578.95	0.00	$1,605.74
2003	10676.6	24.45	$1,998.36
2004	1148.76	7.61	$2,150.38
2005	16111.43	40.24	$3,015.61
2006	17225.83	6.92	$3,224.20
2007	15307.78	0.00	$3,224.20
2008	8859.56	0.00	$3,224.20
2009	10546.44	19.04	$3,838.09

FIGURE 2.2

Amazing, isn't it? By simply eliminating the losses and making them zero, the performance of this particular index went from a 79-percent loss to a 284-percent gain. And just so you don't miss what a wide margin of difference that represents, the $3,838.09 in this hypothetical "no loss" scenario is 1,668 percent more money than the $217.13 in the first (and actual) example.

As significant as that difference is, you may be saying, "Sure, throw in four years with +20-percent gains, with no losses along the way, and that will always be a big number."

But to show you that it really does have more to do with eliminating losses than it does with making big returns, let's look at that same time period again, continuing to eliminate the losing years, but this time capping the maximum growth in any of those nine positive years to just 7 percent.

Nikkei 225 Index with No Loss Years and a 7% Maximum Cap on Annual Gains

YEAR	END OF YEAR CLOSE	GAIN OR LOSS	VALUE AT YEAR END
1989	38,915.90	NA	$1,000.00
1990	23,848.70	0.00	$1,000.00
1991	22,983.80	0.00	$1,000.00
1992	16,925.00	0.00	$1,000.00
1993	17,417.20	2.91	$1,029.08
1994	19,723.10	7.00	$1,101.12
1995	19,868.20	0.74	$1,109.22
1996	19,361.30	0.00	$1,109.22
1997	15,258.70	0.00	$1,109.22
1998	13,842.17	0.00	$1,109.22
1999	18,934.34	7.00	$1,186.86
2000	13,785.69	0.00	$1,186.86
2001	10,542.60	0.00	$1,186.86
2002	8,578.95	0.00	$1,186.86

2003	10,676.60	7.0	$1,269.94
2004	11,488.76	7.0	$1,358.84
2005	16,111.43	7.0	$1,453.96
2006	17,225.83	6.92	$1,554.53
2007	15,307.78	0.00	$1,554.53
2008	8,859.56	0.00	$1,554.53
2009	10,546.44	7.00	$1,663.34

FIGURE 2.3

You see what I mean? Protecting against loss really can be more significant than trying to swing for the fences. Even if we hypothetically capped the annual gains in this example to a maximum of 7 percent (as seen in figure 2.3), it would still have provided an ending value of $1,663, which represents 514 percent more money than the index actually produced — even with those four years of big annual gains.

I am a firm believer that protecting your downside, so you never have to try to make back the losses you experience in negative market years, is the key to long-term success. And fortunately, as you have certainly gathered by now, that is easily achievable in today's marketplace. And, it's achievable without having to give up positive returns in the years that the market has positive gains.

AVERAGE RETURNS TELL AN ACCURATE STORY

M Y T H   3

Here's the scoop: most stock market benchmarks (indexes as they are called, like the Dow Jones Industrial, the S&P 500, the Russell 2000), as well as most mutual funds, tout their average returns over given periods of time. One year, three years, five years, and a lifetime. They post them on their fact sheets. They share them with the media. In my opinion, it's what most (dare I say, all) financial professionals preach to their clients.

"Yes, Mr. and Mrs. Client, the S&P 500 has returned an average of 10.16 percent over the last 20 years, even when you include the terrible results of 2008."[VIII]

Hogwash! The statement may be factually true, but in reality, it's misleading — worthless.

Why? Simple. There is a huge difference between the average return and the actual return. To illustrate, I'm going to ask you a question. A question that, at first glance, seems ridiculously simple. Silly even. But this question could be one of the most powerful concepts you could grasp in order to take control of your financial future. Here it is:

If a person invests $1,000 into an account and this account experiences a negative 50-percent return in year one and a positive 50-percent return in year two, how much money would be in the account at the end of the second year?

Think about it for a second. The average return is zero, right?

$$\frac{(-50\%) + 50\%}{2} = \frac{0}{2} = 0\% \text{ AVERAGE}$$

YEAR 1   YEAR 2

FIGURE 3.1

Well, if the **average** return is zero percent (which it is), then wouldn't the ending value be equal to its beginning value of $1,000?

Nope. Not even close.

The average return may be zero percent, but the actual return is negative 25 percent!

What!? How can that be?

Let me illustrate using the numbers. If a person invests $1,000 into an account, and in the first year, it experiences a negative 50-percent return, then that $1,000 drops to $500, correct?

$1,000 less 50% = $500
($500)

FIGURE 3.2
50% of $1,000 is $500.

Now, if that account has a positive 50-percent gain in year two, it would increase back up to $750.

$500 plus 50% = $750
($250)

FIGURE 3.3
50% of $500 is $250. $500 + $250 = $750

So, at the end of two years, even though the average return is zero percent, the account actually experienced a 25-percent drop.

How can this be true? If the average return is zero, how can the ending value be significantly less? Why aren't these values the same? It's very simple:

The "actual" return and the "average" return will NEVER equal one another anytime you have to factor in a negative number.

In other words, if you ever have to factor in a negative year's result (the year in which a market went down), then the average return (the number often boasted to the public) and the actual return (the amount that an account or fund actually experienced) will never be the same.

Since markets do experience negative years, the averaging method just doesn't work. It's not an accurate picture of how a market or account has really performed — unless, of course, every year during that period has experienced a positive return.[IX]

Why is this important? Because, if you can employ a strategy that never has to factor in a loss — a negative number — then you will no longer suffer from this myth. That's because the average return and the actual return in that portfolio would be exactly the same.

YOU CAN EFFECTIVELY MANAGE YOUR OWN PORTFOLIO

MYTH 4

The Internet has created an endless list of new phenomena in the past two decades, and some of these changes have been so gradual and so pervasive that we have lost sight of just how far things have moved from what we once knew. Here are just a few examples:

It wasn't long ago that you had no choice but to battle the crazed mall parking lots during the Christmas season in order to buy gifts for all on your list; now, it just takes a few clicks on your home computer while you're watching your favorite television show. Ten years ago, you had to take your car to a mechanic to get it fixed; now, just a short, step-by-step, YouTube video will do. It seems like only yesterday that music CDs were the hottest way to buy music; now, it's simply a click to download. Or, what about a college degree? Only a few years ago, you had to attend class at an actual college to get a degree; now, you can get one from the comfort of your own home.

These Internet phenomena have built within us the belief that we can figure out everything on our own with just a few clicks of a keyboard, and that we don't need others' advice, counsel, or help. I believe this is terribly unwise. We are not qualified in all areas to "do-it-ourselves." We are in some things, certainly, like repairing cars, Christmas shopping, and learning piano — all of which can save us time, money and travel, and contribute positively to our lives. But, there are other areas in which these over-confident, "do-it-yourself" Internet phenomena can prove quite dangerous. And in no area more so than personal finance. I do understand that many good tools exist, so it isn't so much that we *can't* do it ourselves; rather, it's more that we *shouldn't* do it ourselves.

Why do I believe this so strongly? Two words: human nature. In my opinion, we are wired incorrectly when it comes to managing our own money. And, I'm not sure this is changeable even if we do recognize the magnitude of our shortcomings. Why? Because, we can't rewire our inborn nature or our need for "fight or flight." That is hardwired from our first breath. And, when it comes to money and the markets, this innate desire for "fight or flight" may morph into two slightly different words: greed and fear. Now, you may be thinking, "'Fight or flight' doesn't sound anything like 'greed and fear.'" But I assure you they are. And, if they are not brothers from the same set of parents, they are certainly cousins who share the same grandparents.

I believe the instinctive reaction for greed and fear in the markets is simply an adaptation of our ancestral need for "fight or flight." Think about it. What does our "fight or flight" nature cause us to do? It prompts us to jump in and duke it out (either figuratively or non-figuratively) when we see a chance of winning, or it urges us to turn and run, and escape when danger is imminent.

Isn't that also true of the markets? How many individuals wrongly jumped into the equity ring, ready to duke it out and conquer some massive profits, during the insanely overstretched technology bubble of the late 90s. I, unfortunately, was one of those who put on my "market gloves" and jumped into the ring. You can read about this disaster in my first book, *Tax-Free Retirement*. As a matter of fact, it was this experience that led me to seek out new, safer strategies for long-term wealth accumulation; I never wanted to experience that kind of loss ever again.

How many times have individuals liquidated their equity holdings after experiencing massive losses? Just look at 2008 and 2009 for a clear picture. People lined up to exit the equity markets en masse for fear of losing it all. They didn't know where the bottom would settle, and they didn't want to find out. So they bailed. Fear caused them to run. Isn't this simply our inherent "flight" mechanism adapted to our high-tech, financial world? All of our receptors are screaming at us to flee. Run. Get away. Leave while there is at least something still intact.

You see, while "fight or flight" may serve us well when it comes to survival, greed and fear do *not* serve us well when it comes to our finances. In fact, they can prompt exactly the wrong decision at exactly the wrong time. And that can be an explosive, and often expensive, combination.

Let me share an analogy of how greed and fear work, and why they are so destructive to our financial well-being.

Picture a large, remote ranch in the wilds of Wyoming — a place of endless skies and snow-capped mountains. On this particular ranch lives a man who rescues, cares for, and trains wild horses that roam the land and need a place to call home.

One day, this rancher looks out his kitchen window and sees a massive herd of wild mustangs standing just outside the gate to one of his corrals. Horses he's watched and admired for years.

Without scaring the herd away, the rancher goes out

to the pen and opens the gate as wide as it will open. He places food in the center of the corral and hopes some of these mustangs will make their way in.

And, they begin to do exactly that. Just a minute later, two of the skinny horses, hungry for sustenance, make their way into the corral and begin eating.

"Wow! Two already!" mumbles the rancher to nobody but himself.

He stands and watches as a couple more get close to the gate. His heart beats a little faster. He says to the horses, as if they can understand him, "C'mon guys. Follow 'em in. There's only love and a good home here. Don't be scared." And sure enough, they do.

Then three more walk toward the pen. The rancher feels the excitement build in his chest as if something has come alive. "If these three go in, I'll have seven. That's incredible!" And sure enough, they do. Then number eight walks in, followed by number nine.

Now, here's where greed causes the rancher to make his first mistake. Nine horses would be his best rescue ever. More than double his previous best. But, does he shut the corral gate, content to add nine horses to his ranch? No. Why? Because there are still more standing out in the field that have not made their way in, and the rancher doesn't want to shut the gate if he has the opportunity to acquire more horses. Greed has begun to whisper in his ear, "Don't shut the gate now. Number ten will be along very soon. If you shut the gate, you'll miss out on that additional gain." So, he leaves the pen wide open.

And, as he is waiting for horse number ten to make his

way into the pen, number nine turns away from the feed and walks out. Where there once stood nine horses feeding in the middle of his corral there now stand only eight. The rancher's heart sinks a little. "Dang! I should have closed the gate when there were nine. Now there are only eight. I definitely can't shut the gate now, because number nine is certain to walk back in. And when he does, and I get back to nine horses, then I'll shut the gate and call it good."

However, as he watches and waits, instead of number nine walking back in, number eight walks out. And, now he's down to seven horses.

The rancher's heart sinks deeper. Now, he's frustrated with himself. He laments. "Why didn't I lock up at least the eight horses? That was more than enough. Now, I only have seven. Okay, this time, I promise myself that as soon as one of those two horses walks back into the corral, I'll close the gate and be done — content with that."

But it doesn't happen. Instead, as he's waiting for just one of the two horses to walk back in, number seven walks out. Then number six, then five and four and three and two and one. And before long, the corral stands completely empty.

After each horse walks out, the rancher repeats the same promise to himself, over and over and over again. He keeps promising himself that as soon as just one of the horses walks back in, he'll shut the gate and be done. But, it never happens. Instead, he watches every last horse walk out of the pen, join back up with the herd, and head back into the wild.

What was the rancher's downfall? Greed. Not a bad greed or an evil greed. Simply a sense of wanting just a little more, instead of being content with what he'd already gained and locking in the ones he'd already acquired.

This is the same manner in which some people react when it comes to the equity markets. They want just a little more, so they stay in, never locking in their profits. Then, when the markets experience a rough patch — as markets always do — they hold on tight and ride the losses down, promising themselves all along the way that as soon as their accounts get back to where they once were, they will shut the gate and be done. But during times of extreme and negative volatility, their accounts often don't rise quickly back to where they once stood; rather, they continue their nose-dive into the depths. And, at some point, like we saw in 2008 and 2009, the pain gets so severe, and the fear gets so real, that their natural response is to bail. Run for cover. Protect what they have. So, they liquidate everything at prices ridiculously lower than they once experienced. And, sometimes, those losses are steep.

Then, often, since they exited due to fear, they stand on the sidelines as the markets make their long, upward recovery, missing out on any chance to make back some of the losses they suffered.

It's greed and fear, prompting the wrong response at every step. Unfortunately, that seems to be our nature when it comes to managing our own money. We are too enmeshed with it to detach ourselves from letting greed and fear lead us astray.

This is one of the primary reasons I am a strong believer in working with a well-trained, fully licensed, financial professional. A person who cares a lot about you and your money but is a step further removed from the emotion of it, allowing him or her to make more objective decisions for you, decisions that are less likely to be motivated by greed or fear.

Another reason why I'm a fan of working with this kind of professional is that he or she — if they are up to date on all of the new product offerings in the marketplace — can help you choose the correct path for your specific situation, the right mix that will fit both your goals and your risk tolerance.

And, just in case you haven't been told, there are some exciting new products and strategies that have been launched in the last few years that can allow you to lock in your gains without ever having to watch them vanish. Strategies that work more like a "crab pot" than a horse corral. What I mean by that, for those of you who have never used a crab pot before, is that it is designed with a door that is hinged in one direction. It swings in so the crab may enter the pot, but once in, it can never leave. Once it's in, it's in. The crab fisherman doesn't have to worry about losing his bounty once he's acquired it. He can acquire gains without fear of loss. And the same can be true with some of today's new financial innovations. There is a way to have the gate be "open" for the gains to walk in, yet actively closed so they can't walk out. It's pretty remarkable and easily achievable.

So, just like the previous three myths, it all comes down to protecting your portfolio against loss, yet at the same time, not preventing it from gains. *That* is a winning strategy. Just ask the crab fisherman; he'll tell you.

IF SOMETHING IS REALLY THAT GOOD, EVERYONE WOULD BE DOING IT

MYTH 5 ─────────────────────────────

If there was a car that could protect you from ever getting into an accident, and this car was one you found attractive and in the same price range of another similar quality car without that feature, would you buy it? It seems the answer would be a no-brainer, and you'd jump at the chance. As a matter of fact, you might even think, "If a car was really *that* good, wouldn't everyone be driving it?" But they don't, as reality shows by looking around. Because, in truth, there are cars on the market that offer features that can prevent many (if not most) accidents. Cars that beep if another car is in your blind spot once your turn signal is activated. Cars that park themselves. And, recently, I saw a video for a car that literally drives itself, keeping between the lines on the road, then braking all by itself to prevent an accident. Crazy, but true. As you can see, there has been a vast leap forward in automotive technology, yet most drivers on the road do not drive one of these cars. I'm sure this is often due to pricing, but, other times, I'm sure it's just lack of knowledge that these cars even exist or how dramatically they may improve one's safety on the road.

Cars are not the only product to undergo such amazing innovations. It's happened in nearly all fields, including the financial sector. For instance, if someone told an individual, decades ago, there was a financial product that could potentially give them positive appreciation in the years the market was up and would protect them against loss in the years the market was down, what would their reaction have been? If it wasn't hysterical laughter, it would have at least been complete disbelief. And, that mocking and doubt would have been justified, because such an opportunity didn't exist 25 or 30 years ago. But, fortunately, it does exist today. Yet, sometimes, people still mock and doubt — even in the face of truth. Why? Because sometimes, people mock and doubt what they don't understand or haven't experienced. But, regardless of an individual's personal beliefs, technology marches forward with or without him.

So, what do you think? Do you believe a strategy exists that can give you upside, positive growth, while at the same time protect you against any market downturn? If you don't, then it's likely been far too long since you've met with a qualified individual to find out about all of the incredible financial innovations that have rolled out in the last decade or so. Innovations that allow you to step away from the erroneous thinking that a person must take big risks in order to try and make solid returns.

If the idea of a financial product that can protect you against loss, while still offering growth potential, excites you as much as an automobile that could protect you from a possible accident, then I want to encourage you to do what I encourage everyone to do: Do a little homework, and check out the facts and figures for yourself. Don't just take my word for it. Prove it to yourself. Really, what have you got to lose? A couple hours of time, maybe? But, think of all you stand to gain! The possibility of never having to suffer another loss due to a declining stock market. And, for those of you who weathered both the bursting of the technology bubble and the global, credit meltdown, that may be one very welcome strategy.

IMPORTANT DISCLOSURES

1. This book is not intended to give any investment, legal, or tax advice of any kind. As a matter of fact, this book promises nothing more than an hour of reading. Hopefully *enjoyable* reading. However, if you don't like it, just consider it an inexpensive sleep aid with fewer side effects than prescription meds.

2. The financial product referenced to in this book is a Fixed Indexed Annuity. Fixed Indexed Annuities offer the ability to earn interest based on the performance of a stock market index, such as the S&P 500. Contractual obligations are backed by the financial strength and claims-paying ability of the insurer. Annuities may be subject to limitations and fees that need to be considered before purchasing a contract. The exact terms of the annuity and any riders are contained in the contract.

3. It is important to understand that a Fixed Indexed Annuity is not a securities product.

4. Let me be clear on something. *Nothing* is risk-free. And, while I don't believe I ever make such a statement in this book, I want to be incredibly forthright about that statement. Everything has risk of some kind. Market risk. Inflation risk. Opportunity cost risk. And many other possible types of risks. While Fixed Indexed

Annuities minimize risk in many important areas, they do no eliminate risk altogether. Also any guarantees provided by annuities are subject to the claims-paying ability of the issuing company, which is a risk in itself.

5. Fixed Indexed Annuities, like any financial product, need a full and detailed explanation of their many unique features. In particular, with Fixed Indexed Annuities, the consumer should seek full understanding of such things as "caps," "fees," "spreads," "participation rates," "crediting methodologies," "bonuses," "bonus recapture," and any other feature that a particular product may provide. Again, it is not the intention or scope of this book to detail those items; that should be discussed in a face-to-face meeting with a licensed and knowledgeable representative in your local area.

6. Please know that the terms "safe" and "secure" – when used to describe an insurance product including a Fixed Indexed Annuity – are references to, and based solely upon, the financial strength and claims-paying ability of the issuing company.

It is my hope that this book will simply be a *starting point* in your financial journey. Not an ending point. Please do not make any financial or purchasing decisions – of any kind – based on the words in this book. That should be done only after a thorough and proper conversation with a properly licensed professional. Please know I wish you nothing but the very best, both now and in the years to come.

ENDNOTES ─────────────────────────────

"Standard & Poor's," " S&P 500," "Standard & Poor's 500," and "500" are all registered trademarks of the McGraw-Hill Companies, Inc. These products are not sponsored, endorsed, or sold or promoted by Standard & Poor's, and Standard & Poor's make no representation regarding the advisability of purchasing these products.

I Wikipedia – Bear Stearns (http://en.wikipedia.org/wiki/Bear_Stearns) and Wikipedia – Lehman Brothers (http://en.wikipedia.org/wiki/Lehman_Brothers)

II "86% of the 1955 Fortune 500 have failed." Traderhabits. com. Eli Radke. February 28, 2013. http://traderhabits.com/86-of-the1955-fortune-500-have-failed/

III Past performance is no guarantee of future results. Indices are unmanaged and not available for direct investment. Index returns do not include fees or sales charges. This information is provided for illustrative purposes only and does not reflect the performance of an actual investment.

IV *The Retirement Miracle* by Patrick Kelly, 2011.

V Past performance is no guarantee of future results. Indices are unmanaged and not available for direct investment. Index returns do not include fees or sales charges. This information is provided for illustrative purposes only and does not reflect the performance of an actual investment.

VI CDs and savings accounts are FDIC insured up to $250,000.

VII Wikipedia – Nikkei 225

VIII MoneyChimp.com: http://www.moneychimp.com/
features/market_cagr.htm – based on year-end data
through 2009

ix *The Retirement Miracle* by Patrick Kelly, 2011

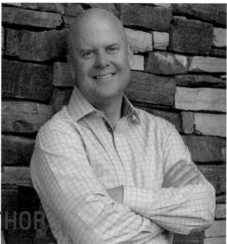

ABOUT THE AUTHOR

Patrick Kelly is the author of three national best-selling books, *Tax-Free Retirement* (2007), *The Retirement Miracle* (2011), and *Stress-Free Retirement* (2013), which together have sold more than 1.5 million copies. Patrick has spent much of his career on a national platform delivering his unique message to over 100,000 advisors from coast to coast and has become one of the industry's most sought-after speakers. Patrick's strong counsel for advisors to practice a "client first" philosophy is the centerpiece of all his messages. One of his greatest passions is to help consumers understand they are able to step off the roller coaster of fear and loss and onto the peace-filled road of growth and stability.

Patrick lives in the Puget Sound area with his wife and their four children.